Praise for *Intimat*

"M. Shahid Alam's elegant rendering of Ghalib's poetry will delight its readers. It will acquaint them with the sensibilities and abstract vision of one of Urdu language's greatest poets, which the translator has ably captured in a fluid language. This book will make a wonderful introduction for the students of world poetry, and claim a prominent place among the few excellent translations of Urdu classical poetry."

—Musharraf Ali Farooqi
translator of *The Adventures of Amir Hamza* by Ghalib Lakhnavi and Abdullah Bilgrami

"Through the experimentations of many poets—including Adrienne Rich, Agha Shahid Ali, and John Hollander—the ghazal, with roots in Arabic, Persian, and Urdu courtly traditions, has proven to be a resilient poetic form that offers new possibilities in our postmodern age. In its very structure, where each couplet is isolated, the ghazal embodies an antithesis to the age-long Western ideal of organic unity so valued by thinkers from Aristotle through Hegel. The ghazal's willful discontinuity harmonizes with our most recent ways of looking at the world through the lens of irreducible particularism. M. Shahid Alam's renderings of Ghalib bring to the fore these rich possibilities of the ghazal as an instrument of irony, self-consciousness, and humor. For example, one couplet of Ghalib translated literally might look like this: 'These problems of Sufism, and this your account, Ghalib— / A saint we'd think you, were you not given to wine!' Alam recreates the verse as follows: 'Ghalib dazzles his fans with his Sufi talk. / He has a chance at sainthood if he sobers up.' This is not just a translation but a reimagining of the entire rhetorical situation, bringing Ghalib's performance—his verse in all its orality—into the 21ˢᵗ century. This book goes a long way not only to redefining Ghalib but also to reconfiguring the immense potential of the ghazal as a new cadence in Western ears."

—M.A.R. Habib
Professor of English, Rutgers University

"M. Shahid Alam's translations of Ghalib are brilliant flashes of poetic illumination. Again and again, they convey the rich polyvalence of the original ghazals—from metaphysical insights to wordplays. His work brings to life the Divan's meanings and forms in poems reminiscent of the Urdu ghazal in their tenor and English lyric in their resonance. Alam has read Ghalib religiously over decades and is an accomplished poet of English in his own right—both these traits are reflected in the exquisite gems bound in this volume. Alam's acumen as a translator-poet is breathtaking, and this volume is a gift to world literature."

—Taimoor Shahid
translator of *The Madness of Waiting* by Muhammad Hadi Ruswa

Intimations of Ghalib

M. Shahid Alam

With a foreword by *Guy Rotella*

ISBN: 978-1-949039-19-1

Orison Books
PO Box 8385
Asheville, NC 28814
www.orisonbooks.com

Distributed to the trade by Itasca Books
1-800-901-3480 / orders@itascabooks.com

Manufactured in the U.S.A.

ORISON
BOOKS

I will have sweet patience.
Qur'an: 12,83

In memory of my son
M. Junaid Alam
1983–2014

Contents

Acknowledgments

Some of these translations have appeared in the journals below; revised versions appear in this volume.

Beloit Poetry Journal – "Suitors"
Blackbird – "Gory," "Collar," "Quarry," "Shroud"
Chicago Review – "Drop," "Artist"
Circumference – "Limits," "Love-Crazed"
Critical Muslim – "Bliss," "Confidant," "Fire"
Kenyon Review – "Mentor," "Registry"
Michigan Quarterly Review – "Qays"
Mudlark – "Ash'aar"
Notre Dame Review – "Perilous," "Goodbye"
Paintbrush – "Férhad"
Prairie Schooner – "Houris," "Kaaba," "Mercy"
Raritan – "Jesus," "Paradise," "Man"
Salamander – "Impaled"
Salt River Review – "Sightless"
Southern Review – "Afterlife," "Charmers," "Maelstrom"
TriQuarterly Review – "God," "Uncoffined"
Western Humanities Review – "Headstone," "Song"

Foreword

I first encountered Ghalib in the early 1970s. I was in graduate school, studying poetry. Then, as now, I had no Urdu. The medium of transmission—translation—was Aijaz Ahmad's *Ghazals of Ghalib*, from Columbia University Press. It comprised versions of ghazals by W.S. Merwin, Adrienne Rich, William Stafford, Mark Strand, and others, all of them working from Ahmad's literal translations and supplementary comments. My interest (probably slaking along the way some ersatz thirst for the supposedly exotic) was more in the American poets I admired than in the original poems they tried to bring into English. Merwin, Rich, and the rest were driven to Ghalib, or so I thought, by their quest for alternative models to the high modernist masters they were trying to shed or shred, by their search for remoter precedents to replace nearer ones they needed to reject.

The ghazal is united by form (two-line units, rigorous patterns of rhyme and refrain) but discontinuous in theme (each two-line stanza is distinct and separable from its fellows). The ghazal is also oral and performative, even in some ways interactive. And, however much it is steeped in tradition, at least in Ghalib's hands, it feels intensely personal. This must have seemed an antidote to imaginations trained on, then sick of the thematic and other unities of British and American poems, of the primacy of print, and of the then still thunderous mandate to write impersonally that had begun as a revolt and become an orthodoxy. There's irony in this: the ghazal belongs to a master-apprentice tradition bound not only to technical rigor but also to stern commitments to inherited and formulaic sets of images, characters, and motifs. But it's an irony lightened by the ghazal's roots in oral performance and by the at least apparent likeness of its discontinuities to the surrealist, deep image, and other, often foreign styles American poets in those days were trying out and trying on. At a time of cultural upheaval, when America's inherited colonial war in Vietnam was being prosecuted and protested, Ghalib's particular circumstances might have resonated, too. He was an impecunious aristocrat in a still only nascently nationalist India; he lived at the tag end of a dying Mughal dynasty increasingly beholden to British colonial rulers who were capable of monstrous reprisals to repress and punish rebellion; he could seem to have made a separate peace. A faithful but non-sectarian Muslim, Ghalib was also wittily, irascibly irreverent and more in tune with ecstatic Sufi sensuality than more conservative Islamic asceticism, as much given to the pleasures of love affairs and wine as to those of the strictest poetic craft. Even Ghalib's more than Keatsian precocity—many of his finest poems were written by the time he was 19—might have seemed a recommendation in those youth-besotted days.

However all of that may be, the poems Stafford, Strand, and others made from Ahmad's versions were refreshing, part of a burgeoning culture of alternative inspirations and excitements. How much they conveyed of Ghalib is another matter. (Thirty years later, Robert Bly, another American poet of the Rich and Merwin generation, had his own, more thoroughgoing try, working once more from literal translations, this time done by Sunil Dutta.)

Meanwhile, my awareness of Ghalib lay dormant. Then, several years ago, I received a note from a university colleague I didn't know (Shahid Alam, a professor of Economics). He asked, with unusual courtesy, if I'd look at some verse translations he'd been working on. I said I would. I'm very glad I did. Those poems initiated a valued friendship, and proved to be among the splendid versions of Ghalib's ghazals in English collected in this book. Of course I can't properly estimate the fidelity of Alam's translations to their Persian-inflected Urdu sources, any more than I could that of the earlier ones I've mentioned, but I know Shahid Alam is fluent in Urdu and has made very good poems in English. I'm also sure that his versions carry over into English unusually many of the formal properties that give the ghazal its particular excellence, character, value, and flavor: not only the disruptive thematic disunity and soothingly constant formulaic repertoire already mentioned (and the combined tension and release that pairing produces) but also its wealth of rhyme and refrain, its seriousness and wit, and its typically dramatic first and self-referential final distich. Most of the biographical and technical information necessary to appreciate the poems is given in the translator's introduction. It remains for me to point out a few of these poems' manifold successes.

In contrast with English, Urdu is a highly abstract, multivalent, and richly suggestive language (whatever English's connotative resources, alongside Urdu it can seem narrowly concrete and specific). One way Alam represents those qualities of Ghalib's originals is by offering multiple versions of particular poems, usually two, once as many as five, a device that helps convey Urdu's and the poems' great range of expressive and interpretative potential. For instance, two versions of the same ghazal (here numbered 24.1 and 24.2) variously mock, rage against, and humbly accept divine control of human life and death.

Ghazals are by definition love poems. They address loved ones both secular and sacred, and they consider persons, events, situations, and feelings of every conceivable type and kind: the beloved may be coy, disdainful, or yielding; love may be requited, refused, or ignored; love might persist or go stale, or—in ecstasy or departure—take flight; lovers in ghazals can experience joy, contentment, satiety, boredom, indifference, anger, despair, or hate, sometimes several of them all at once. And because Urdu pronouns don't distinguish gender or separate the human from the divine, other possibilities ramify. All of this gives Ghalib's verse, to borrow English literary terms, Petrarchan, mock-Petrarchan, and Metaphysical qualities. Love is infinitely intense, a tempest or shower of arrows; yet love's "grand gestures" can be ridiculed, ridiculous. Meanwhile, this superb and superbly rendered pair of lines matches anything in Donne:

> Shaped for eternity: yet tied to time's cross.
> What did he think whose hand crafted us?

As the opening lines of the poem numbered 35.4, this passage also captures the dramatic quality characteristic of a ghazal's initial stanza: here, the tension generated when statement confronts interrogation, when the meanings embedded in the word "think" shift and multiply, when the vowel sounds in "cross" and "us" diversify and echo. Alam is a master of assonance. He uses it, as well as more straightforward rhyme and repetition, to convey in English a good deal—if, inevitably, far from all—of the formal patterning ghazals entail. As mentioned, refrains are required. In poem 30 the word "free" is repeated at the end of every other line, and in such a way as to deploy many of the myriad shades of meaning that vital word contains; among other things, the device reminds us that freedom within constraint is the hallmark of successful formal verse. Other sorts of excellence abound. Here is an instance of Ghalib's masterfully discreet yet explicit sensuality, masterfully conveyed:

> All day, the Seven Sisters stay veiled, out of sight.
> What is it that makes them bare it all by night?

And here, from the poem 2.2 (Charmers) is a potent pun: "Beyond creeds and rites we worship God alone." The final word indicates independence and loneliness both; it can apply, in grandeur and desolation, to both worshipper and worshipped.

Alam captures well Ghalib's aristocratic hauteur and often self-deprecating humor, his comic mixtures of lofty and demotic diction, and his quick shifts of mood and tone: when Alam writes "I have laughed at my lows. / Now nothing lifts me," the incomplete chiastic structure communicates the drastic, stomach-churning drop from confident boast to hollow despair (and perhaps as well the tears that would complete the low-high, laughing-crying chiastic cross). Alam is equally adept at finding equivalents for Ghalib's often densely ideational imagery, as in these intellectually teasing lines on containment's capacity to be both a claustrophobic trap and a liberatingly vast expanse:

> Inside the heart, love carps it lacks space.
> Inside a pearl, the raging sea is free.

Or consider the all-but Gordian knot of these faithful, heretical, mystifying, utterly lucid lines:

> Love-crazed yet craving life. I worship fire
> But recant when lightning finds me out.

The translator's play with the like and unlike sounds of "crazed" and "craving," the similar but divergent images of fire and lightning, and the related and opposed ideas of worship and recanting is an ongoing revelation. Finally, as an English-language reader, I much enjoy the way these poems combine formal unity with thematic disunity to build and maintain or resolve the tension between sameness and difference that is one of art's enduring pleasures. Perhaps that's a projection of alien expectations on these marvelous poems. Translation loses things, and readers from outside a writer's culture lose a great deal more. But translators help us recover some of what we've lost or otherwise could never have at all. I'm thankful to Shahid Alam for bringing so much of Ghalib's world and the world of the ghazal to the English page. I think other readers will be grateful, too.

Guy Rotella
Emeritus Professor of English Literature
Northeastern University, Boston

Ghalib: Introduction

Ghalib is the poetic name (Urdu, *takhallus* / تّخَلُص) of Mirza Asadullah Baig Khan. Unlike the pen name that commonly conceals a writer's identity, the takhallus is chosen to reveal the persona of the poet; more often than not, an Urdu poet is known by his takhallus. The poet's first takhallus was Asad ("lion"). When he discovered that another poet was writing under this takhallus, he changed his to Ghalib ("vanquisher").

Ghalib was born in Agra in 1797 into a family that held revenue rights to land in return for military services; his father and uncle died fighting for their paymasters. He was married at thirteen, moved to Delhi in 1810 and, except for an absence of three years that took him to Kolkata, he never left the city—not even during the rebellion of 1857 or its aftermath when the British excluded Muslims from Delhi for two years—and died there in 1869. As an aristocrat, he considered it below his dignity to hold a job—and once turned down a chance to teach Persian at Delhi College, ostensibly because the college Principal did not show sufficient deference to his noble status when he showed up for the interview —and his only steady source of income was his share of the pension his uncle's heirs received from the British colonial rulers. This income was supplemented in his later years by the patronage of the last nominal head of the Mughal dynasty—now confined to Delhi at the pleasure of the British East India Company—and gifts from the Nawab of Rampur. His panegyrics to colonial administrators—including one to Queen Victoria—written in hopes of patronage never paid off.

Ghalib's poetic reputation rests primarily on his slim Urdu divan or collection of ghazals (in Urdu script, singular, غَزَل, plural, غَزَلِیں). This is ironic for several reasons. Muhammad Sadiq, author of *A History of Urdu Literature* (1964), has written with some exaggeration that Ghalib's Urdu poetry "was merely an accident in his career and forms a very small fraction of his works." Many of the ghazals in his Urdu divan were written in his teens; after 1821 he began to compose in Persian and from then on wrote only occasionally in Urdu. Although Ghalib has written that his Urdu ghazals are "colorless" compared to his "colorful" Persian ghazals, few critics take him at his word. It is more likely that he saw more honor in joining the pantheon of classical Persian poets of Iran and India. Although Urdu poetry had been gaining in popularity among India's nobility, it lacked the prestige of Persian, the chief literary language of the Indo-Persian world for several centuries.

Ghalib's poetic genius had blossomed early. Most of his Urdu ghazals were written in his teens and twenties, and they equal or surpass the later additions to his Urdu divan. This proved lucky for him and the millions of acolytes of Urdu poetry. In the decades following 1837, when the British replaced Persian with English as the official language of India, Urdu and Hindi slowly replaced it in literary discourse as well. Had it not been for Ghalib's slim Urdu divan and his Urdu letters, Ghalib may have been no better known than the other great Persian poets of South Asia, Khusrau, Nazeeri, Urfi, Fayzi, and Bedil.[1]

Underappreciated in his life, Ghalib's standing among critics and aficionados of the Urdu ghazal continued to rise in the decades after his death. By late nineteenth century, he was being acclaimed by many as India's greatest poet of Urdu and Persian. In addition, the publication of collections of his letters in Urdu brought him recognition as the greatest stylist of Urdu prose as well. In a poem he wrote in 1906, Muhammad Iqbal—the greatest poet of Urdu in the 20th

---

1   According to Frances Pritchett, *Desertful of Roses,* her web-archive of commentaries on Ghalib, Ghalib's Urdu divan consists of some 1459 ash'aar.

century—compares Ghalib to Goethe. In 1921, Abdur Rehman Bijnori, a leading literary critic of the time, wrote, "There are only two divinely revealed books in India: the sacred *Vedas* and *Divan-e-Ghalib*." Another critic, Rasheed Ahmad Siddiqui, declared that the Mughals had bestowed three enduring legacies on India: Urdu, Ghalib and the Taj.

Few literary forms in use today have a more ancient lineage than the ghazal. It first appeared as the amatory prelude to the Arabic ode—*qaseeda*—in pre-Islamic times. Quite early on, however—during the Umayyad era—the ghazal was emancipated from the qaseeda to become a major literary genre in its own right. It was soon taken up by the Persian poets, and under their influence the ghazal passed into Turkish, Urdu, and other languages. Only in Urdu, however, most major poets have continued to write ghazals into the 20th and 21st centuries; they have also introduced new themes and new vocabulary without altering its form or displacing its classical heritage. In part because of this vitality of contemporary ghazals, the leading contemporary Urdu poets still have legions of admirers that would be the envy of poets in almost any other language. Although the tradition of singing ghazals existed in the 19th century as well—when it was sung mostly by courtesans—since the 1950s this musical genre gained both in popularity and prestige as it was integrated into the classical musical traditions of South Asia. Its incorporation into the musical repertoire of Urdu and Hindi films helped to extend its popularity and introduce it to new audiences in South Asia even outside of Hindi and Urdu-speaking circles.

A ghazal consists of an arrangement of very short poems (singular, *sh'er*, plural, *ash'aar*), each consisting of two lines (*misr'a*, singular, *misr'e*, plural). Characteristic of these ash'aar is the contrast between their prosodic unity and (nearly always) their thematic disunity.[2] All the lines in a ghazal have the same length and follow the same meter, while the second line of each sher ends in an identical refrain (*radeef*), consisting of a word or phrase, that is preceded by a rhyming word (*qaafia*). Both lines of the ghazal's opening sher (*matla*) follow this pattern of refrain and rhyme. In addition, the poet incorporates his takhallus in the last sher (*maqta*) of the ghazal.[3] The insertion of the takhallus gives the poet freedom to engage in play-acting, situating himself in many different roles, addressing himself in the third person, making observations on his relations with his beloved, rival or rivals in love, patron, critic, mentor, or God. It is a powerful device for creating ironic distance between the poet and what he says about himself, his interlocutors, his times, and his surroundings.

Nearly always, the sher possesses an internal two-part movement. The first line establishes a tension by posing a question, proposing an enigma, enunciating a mystery, or raising an expectation (for instance, by making an unfinished statement that demands completion) which the second line then resolves, explains, or completes. Alternatively, the two lines of a sher may appear as two independent statements, thus inviting or challenging the reader to discover hidden connections between them. In order to heighten this tension, poets and singers repeat the first line (*misra*) of each sher multiple times; this repetition also encourages the listeners, and as well gives them time, to speculate about what the second line might deliver. Indeed, a poet in the audience may attempt to complete the sher in his own mind; the rhyme-refrain pattern of the ghazal encourages such audience participation in the poetic experience of the ghazal. In the second line, the poet seeks to dazzle his

---

2   A. J. Arberry described a ghazal as "Oriental pearls at random strung." A. J. Arberry, "Oriental Pearls at Random Strung," *Bulletin of the School of Oriental and African Studies*, 11(1946): 699-712.

3   Many writers in English translate sher as "couplet" or "distich." This is misleading since the two lines in a couplet or distich rhyme, and generally a couplet or distich cannot be read independently of the poem of which it is a part.

audience by the manner in which he resolves the tension created by the first line. A sh'er may move the audience to raptures by the force and beauty of surprise delivered by the second line. There are endless ways in which the second line may complete, complement, explicate, enhance, alter, or reverse the meaning and force of the first line.

The centrality of the ghazal across so many languages and so many centuries points to the enduring vitality of this genre. How are we to explain this vitality? A form that makes so many prosodic demands could not have flourished as a major poetic vehicle if Arabic, Persian, Turkish, and Urdu did not have the linguistic resources to meet these demands. At the same time, it should be noted that the ghazal makes fewer prosodic demands than the English sonnet. In particular, while the sonnet is restricted to a specific meter and line length, the ghazal is free from these restrictions. Poets of the ghazal are free to choose from a wide range of meters and line lengths in order to match its music with the mood of the ghazal.

No poetic form, especially one that is as structured as the ghazal, can endure without a robust creative tension between the form of the ghazal and its content. A restrictive prosody succeeds only when it disciplines the poet's imagination even as it spurs him or her to appropriate and create the linguistic and literary resources that expand his or her powers of expression. Over the first few centuries of the ghazal's journey, the poets of the ghazal created a rich literary culture with its own vocabulary, conventions, devices, stories, images, metaphors, symbols, and dramatis personae drawn from the history, traditions, and ecologies of the Middle East. As the different elements of this world of the ghazal came into place, as the familiarity of the readers with the different elements of this culture increased, poets of the ghazal could adumbrate complex structures of meaning in a single sh'er using the rich vocabulary of the ghazal. Once this shared culture was in place, the poet could quickly summon rich associations and clusters of meaning with brief references to the characters, images, symbols, and situations from this cultural world. As a genre, the ghazal represents a vast, never-ending conversation, amongst a multitude of dramatis personae, that occurs across poets, across generations, and even across languages.

The ghazal began as an amatory prelude to the qaseeda. Once it broke free of its origins, the structure of the ghazal itself—which allowed each sh'er to carve out its own world of meaning independent of the rest of the ghazal—encouraged the poet of the ghazal to incorporate other aspects of life into the ghazal, including the mystical, philosophical, worldly, and political. In addition, while the poets of the ghazal did not generally abandon its amatory core, they developed a language that endowed the amatory ash'aar with ambiguity so that "beloved" of the ghazal could be a young man, friend, a patron, a saint, or God. The poet also introduced greater complexity into amatory situations by populating this discourse with other dramatis personae. In addition to the lover and the beloved, the lover/poet may also address his rivals in love (raqeeb), door-man or gate-keeper of the beloved's house (darbaan), messenger (qaasid), an overzealous mentor (nasih), a censorious preacher (shaikh or wa'ez), executioner (jallad), saint (wali), a judge (qaazi), or ruler (haakim). In other words, the lover does not exist in splendid isolation with his amatory passions, but has to negotiate the vicissitudes of everyday life too even as he deals with the agonies and joys of his amatory life.

The ghazal also embodies traditions of dissent in Islamic discourse, taking positions that are critical of religious orthodoxy both in theology and practice. Not infrequently, the poet of the ghazal gently mocks the representatives of outward religion, speaks openly of neglecting religious duties, and even celebrates his flouting of religious edicts. In other words, insulated by the ambiguity of poetic discourse, the ghazal constituted a zone of free speech in traditional Islamic societies. It is doubtful if poetry in traditional Christian societies—before the Enlightenment—offered a similar space for the expression of dissenting ideas without arousing the ire of religious authorities.

Orality has nearly always been an integral part of the culture of the Urdu ghazal. It was common for a patron, king, prince, or other notable, to convene a gathering of poets (in Urdu, *mushaʾera*) in the night at which each poet would recite, chant or sing (without any musical accompaniment) his ghazal, sometimes a ghazal composed for the occasion in the meter chosen by the patron. At these sessions, the audience including the other poets express their appreciation of a line verbally, with loud *vah, vah* (comparable in spirit to shouts of "bravo" at the end of a concert) or by repeating the line. Sometimes, the audience demands that the poet repeat the sheʾr (in Urdu, *muqarrar irshaad*). Frequently, these sessions continue into the late hours of the night. This tradition is still alive in India, Pakistan, and the Urdu diaspora. Sometimes mushaʾeras are broadcast on radio or television or, when convened before large audiences, their recordings are broadcast on radio and television or made available online.

Translating poetry is hard enough, but it gets harder still when it involves languages belonging to different civilizations. The intricate prosody of the ghazal poses an additional set of challenges: how much of its structure should one, or can one, transfer into English? On top of all this, the translator of Ghalib—perhaps more than translators of other poets of the ghazal—faces the daunting task of conveying at least some of the multiple readings of his ashʾaar.

These very real difficulties have not deterred translators.

8

The intellectual and emotional range and intensity, the linguistic dazzle, delightful playfulness, daring skepticism, and remarkable memorability of Ghalib's finest ash'aar are immediately engaging and their resonance deepens and expands with repeated hearings and readings. Such richness demands to be shared, and, if a few ill-prepared admirers have produced translations so labored, antique, and stilted as to make few converts, others, particularly English-language poets working with native speakers of Urdu, have begun to introduce Ghalib to Western audiences.[4] Most noteworthy among these efforts is a translation project organized by Aijaz Ahmad that assembled a galaxy of English-language poets to translate Ghalib; they included Adrienne Rich, W.S. Merwin, Mark Strand, William Stafford, David Ray, Thomas Fitzsimmons, and William Hunt. These poets worked from literal translations, helpful notes, and commentary provided by Aijaz Ahmad.[5] These translations were first published in 1971 as *Ghazals of Ghalib: Versions from the Urdu* by Columbia University Press. We owe a second book of Ghalib translations, *The Lightning Should Have Fallen on Ghalib*, to Robert Bly and Sunil Dutta, published by HarperCollins in 1999. Notwithstanding what is lost of the originals by the very nature of team translations, some of these translations are works of striking beauty and also convey cadences of the originals. Although some of Robert Bly's translations are a bit prosy, he generally stays closer to the sense of the original ghazals than the poets in Ahmad's *Ghazals of Ghalib*.

Besides these book-length translations by American poets, there are a few occasional translations by a few English-language poets. In 1993, Jane Hirshfield published five translations of Ghalib in an anthology of sacred poetry;

---

4   Although there are—and have been—a few native-speakers of Urdu or others familiar with Urdu in the ranks of English-language poets— among others, Zulfikar Ghose, Agha Shahid Ali, Vijay Seshadri, Anis Shivani—they have yet to produce a book-length translation of Ghalib.

5   Adrienne Rich, W.S. Merwin, and Mark Strand went on to win the Pulitzer Prize in poetry.

they are among the best-crafted translations I have seen so far. She does not name a collaborator on her translations, and I have not been able to determine if she knows any Urdu. Two fine translations of Ghalib's ghazals by Vijay Seshadri, familiar with the original Urdu, are available in his most recent book of poetry, *3 Sections*. Although Agha Shahid Ali published a book of translations from Faiz Ahmed Faiz, *The Rebels' Silhouette*, I am aware of only one translation by him of a ghazal from Ghalib. I should also mention a book by two native-speakers of Urdu, Azra Raza and Sara Goodyear, *Ghalib: Epistemologies of Elegance*, that contains prose translations of twenty of Ghalib's ghazals together with helpful commentary on the translations.[6]

As to the success or failure of my own efforts, others will judge, but I have tried to retain the imagery, metaphors, cadences, conventions, the ghazal's dramatis personae, the two-line format of the sh'er, and the compact appearance of the ghazal on the page.[7] To reflect the many meanings any sh'er or ghazal can generate, in a few cases I have offered two versions of the same original: in one case, as many as five. That said, I make a number of compromises with the ghazal's rhyme-refrain requirements: at times, I reproduce neither; at others, I sacrifice the refrain but retain the rhyme scheme or vice versa; and sometimes I convert the ash'aar in a ghazal into rhyming couplets. Although the ideal I have tried to pursue in my translations is to combine fidelity to the original with poetic qualities in the English version of a sh'er, more often than not this has not been within my reach. In consequence, when I had to choose between thetwo, I have leaned towards the latter; hence, the title of this book, *Intimations of Ghalib*. Always, in this intransigent art of

---

6   Jane Hirshfield, "Ghalib," in Stephen Mitchell, ed., *The Enlightened Heart* (Harper Perennial, 1993): 102-106; Vijay Seshadri, *3 Sections* (Graywolf Press, 2013); Agha Shahid Ali, "Stanzas Shaped by a Ghalib Ghazal," *New England Review* (Spring, 2000): 49; Agha Shahid Ali, *The Rebel's Silhouette: Selected Poems* (University of Massachusetts Press, 1991); Azra Raza and Sara Suleri Goodyear, *Ghalib: Epistemologies of Elegance* (Penguin/Viking, 2009).

transferring poetic values from one language to another, something is lost as something is gained. But translation is an art of compromises: I hope I've made good ones, in tribute to Ghalib, an uncompromised, uncompromising master.

M. Shahid Alam

---

7   Urdu script can expand and contract to produce that appearance; this might be done in English by the manipulation of fonts on a computer, but I've tried to approximate the compact appearance by producing lines of nearly equal length.

Translator's Note

Ghazals lack titles due to the absence of thematic unity. When collected in a divan, ghazals are not numbered, nor does the divan include a table of contents. Instead, they are arranged alphabetically into groups according to the last letter of the refrain (*radeef*) in a ghazal. I have given titles to the English versions only for ease of reference; these consist of some striking word in my English version of the ghazal. Readers familiar with Ghalib's divan may note that I do not generally include all the ash'aar in my English versions. However, nearly always my versions include the first and last ash'aar (*matl'a* and *maqt'a*) of a ghazal.

1 – Afterlife

تسکیں کو ہم نہ روئیں جو ذوقِ نظر ملے
حورانِ خلد میں تری صورت مگر ملے

I did not ask for uncommon beauty in paradise.
Just one that restores the life I had in you.

Slay me, but do not bury me in your yard.
Mad for me, why should the world find you?

I will get around to love's grand gestures too.
When my luck turns, I will be back for you.

Do we have to travel with Khizer for a guide?
I grant he is a sage and looks out for you.

I have called on lovers to look out for Ghalib.
He is disconsolate and languishes like you.

2.1 – Houris

سب کہاں کچھ لالہ و گل میں نمایاں ہو گئیں
خاک میں کیا صورتیں ہوں گی کہ پنہاں ہو گئیں

In roses and tulips they return, but only a few.
How many sages has time stolen from us?

By day, the Seven Sisters hide in veils of light.
At night, in caprice, they unveil before us.

I will have sweet revenge, if our icy charmers
Show up as houris, oh so eager to please us.

She of the moon-bright face and silken hair
Could dazzle our dim nights—if she favored us.

Eyes fixed on the Way, we do not follow rites.
Creeds without dogma bring him closer to us.

With practice, we take our troubles in stride.
Our heaviest sorrows sit lightly upon us.

If Ghalib keeps up this grieving, his sighs
Will gather in clouds, his tears will drown us.

2.2 – Charmers

سب کہاں کچھ لالہ و گل میں نمایاں ہو گئیں
خاک میں کیا صورتیں ہوں گی کہ پنہاں ہو گئیں

Not all, only a few come back to us in tulips.
Many more lie buried, dust on their sleeping eyelids.

All day, the Seven Sisters stay veiled, out of sight.
What is it that makes them bare it all by night?

My eyes pour blood on this night of savage partings.
These lamps shed light to sanctify my sorrow.

We will make them pay for the years of torment,
If, by luck, these sirens are houris in paradise.

Sweet relish of silken nights are his, when she
Unties her jasmine-scented hair in his arms.

I have no use for coy approaches to the divine.
Beyond creeds and rites we worship God alone.

If Ghalib keeps crying inconsolably, your gardens
Will go to seed and weeds will choke your lawns.

3 – Tulip

شبنم بہ گلِ لالہ نہ خالی ز ادا ہے
داغِ دلِ بیدرد نظر گاہِ حیا ہے

As dew on tulips so hangs a tear on beauty's face.
In scars without pain, the heart is in disgrace.

Separation woes are breaking his heart. Once
Green, on her hands the henna leaves grow red.

You do not choose this bondage: it chooses you.
The hand pledging love carves itself in stone.

Cast a glance this way too, world-awaking Sun.
Dark, ominous clouds are drifting over us.

For sins conceived but set aside, credit us,
If we must pay for sins we carry through.

Ghalib, do not grieve if the world snubs you.
When no one favors you, there's God at your side.

4 – Intimacy

یہ نہ تھی ہماری قسمت کہ وصالِ یار ہوتا
اگر اور جیتے رہتے یہی انتظار ہوتا

Fate did not decree that I should be with you.
I would still be waiting if I had more time.

I know that your vows are a clever ruse.
If true and I knew, would I not die of joy?

It is true I prefer your barb inside me.
Would the pain endure if it shot through?

Agony is the inbred discourse of hearts.
The language is the same in love as in life.

Hard on the heart are dark lonely nights.
I do not mind dying, but I die every night.

Who can see the One who is complete? If there
Is room for two where is the point of entry?

Ghalib dazzles the world with his sufi talk.
He has a chance at sainthood if he sobers up.

5 – Gory

هزاروں خواہشیں ایسی کہ ہر خواہش پہ دم نکلے
بہت نکلے مرے ارمان لیکن پھر بھی کم نکلے

One life, many wishes, each to die for slowly.
Many cups overflow, many more lie empty.

Dispatch me: your hands will not be gory.
In tears all night, my blood has left my body.

Adam's exile was never more than a story,
Until she also shut the door on me.

If you want a letter written to her, ask me.
I do it for a living: I have her testimony.

In love, life and death trade places. I die
For a glimpse of one whose glance kills me.

No preacher ever visits a watering hole. Yet,
As I left that place once, I saw him scurry.

6 – Bliss

عشرتِ قطرہ ہے دریا میں فنا ہو جانا
درد کا حد سے گزرنا ہے دوا ہو جانا

A drop craves extinction in the sea.
Past plenitude, pain becomes remedy.

After years I played all the right keys.
In a twist, fate changed the melody.

No one masters his soul without this.
Not mercy, her sword sets us free.

In frailty, my tears turn to sighs.
In clouds, water rises to levity.

I cannot cleave flesh from bone.
I die for your touch: dream inside me.

A cloudburst takes us to clear skies.
After tears, lovers attain felicity.

Ghalib, the tulips quicken discovery.
Open your eyes to all shades of beauty.

7.1 - God

نہ تھا کچھ تو خدا تھا کچھ نہ ہوتا تو خدا ہوتا
ڈبویا مجھ کو ہونے نے نہ ہوتا میں تو کیا ہوتا

My absence was God. If absent, God would be.
If I was not in play, how would that go for me?

I had nothing to lose when she cut off my head.
It lay not on my torso, but dead upon my knee.

Many years after he died, Ghalib comes back to me.
We talked of certainties: *he*, what might have been.

7.2 – God Hereafter

نہ تھا کچھ تو خدا تھا کچھ نہ ہوتا تو خدا ہوتا
ڈبویا مجھ کو ہونے نے نہ ہوتا میں تو کیا ہوتا

God there was before and God hereafter.
What would it matter had I not been?

This beheading was humane. For years
My head lay slumped upon my knee.

His friends recall how Ghalib spoke
Not of now but always what might be.

8 – Qays

شوق ہر رنگ رقیبِ سر و ساماں نکلا
قیس تصویر کے پردے میں بھی عریاں نکلا

The Masters painted him scrawny, naked.
In love's country, Qays travels light.

Scent of roses, sighs, candle smoke: they
That leave her side go broken-hearted.

In a hurry, I scaled the highest peaks.
Now the lesser peaks obstruct me.

Ghalib, a tempest batters my heart.
A tear once repressed troubles my nights.

9 – Jesus

دہر میں نقشِ وفا وجہِ تسلی نہ ہوا
ہے یہ وہ لفظ کہ شرمندۂ معنی نہ ہوا

Love's best laid plans go awry.
Life corrupts us till we die.

I wanted to end love's agony.
She insisted, you dare not die.

I spend my days in the tavern.
I tried piety: it left me dry.

I am strong: be straight with me.
I will not be taken by a lie.

Ghalib was so frail, a breath
Of life caused him to die.

10 – Paradise

ستائش گر ہے زاہد اس قدر جس باغِ رضواں کا
وہ اک گلدستہ ہے ہم بیخودوں کے طاقِ نسیاں کا

In homilies, the preachers hype paradise.
We stopped there once but did not stay.

Drop by drop, she draws blood. In pity
Afterwards, she strings them into beads.

In glory she ignites the hall of mirrors,
As the sun lights up fields of morning dew.

I am compounded of contradictions.
My sparks unify to burn my granary.

Somewhere she sleeps with a lover tonight.
Why else in dreams does she smile so coyly?

This can't be easy. Many hearts will bleed
When she lifts the veil from her grieving eyes.

Ghalib, I have longings of extinction.
This reverie unites the scattered universe.

11 – Quarry

محرم نہیں ہے تو ہی نواہائے راز کا
یاں ورنہ جو حجاب ہے پردہ ہے ساز کا

You stopped just short of the highest note.
Read past the signs crowding the page.

I prepare to die when I start my day.
When she awakes, the world is her stage.

In rapture, you fix your eyes on his face.
Turning on me, they radiate rage.

It's spring! There's a sting in old wounds.
Love tightens its grip, youth vexes age.

A hundred loves lie buried in your heart.
Why dig this quarry, Ghalib? You are a sage.

12 – Sightless

مقدم سیلاب سے دل کیا نشاطِ آہنگ ہے
خانۂ عاشق مگر سازِ صدائے آب تھا

Lake waters rise past the rafters in my house.
Their undulant music calms my rage tonight.

I was homeless before: it was a proper life.
Wine-free, woman-free, I had peace all night.

I was sightless in the cave of desire. Outside,
His light shone brilliantly night after night.

Is this nothing to you, that we live or die?
Time was, our pain kept you up all night.

It happened long ago. Afraid of losing us,
She lifted the veil till her beauty sang all night.

Glad I stopped him. Ghalib was so rattled,
His tears would have drowned the city tonight.

13 – Drop

ایک ایک قطرے کا مجھے دینا پڑا حساب
خونِ جگر و دیعتِ مژگانِ یار تھا

I gave it all back: she wanted every drop of it.
My life-blood was her gift, a trust I kept for years.

I weep among the ruins of the city of desires.
Its lapidary art had mirrored her for years.

Lay down my body when we pass her gate.
My tears have washed these stones for years.

I did not think that love had such force.
When it hit me, I could not sleep for years.

14 – Man

بسکہ دشوار ہے ہر کام کا آساں ہونا
آدمی کو بھی میسّر نہیں انساں ہونا

Was there a time when all things were easy?
Man fails humanity, yet wasn't this easy?

I will be taking my longings to the grave.
Roses and tulips will greet you at my grave.

Come, heighten this pain a notch or two.
If this is dying, give me a death or two.

She buried her sword after she slew me.
Courting in safety, my rivals thank me.

Pity the shirt, Ghalib, on a lover's back.
When he is distraught, he rips it off his back.

15 – Kaaba

کوئی امید بر نہیں آتی
کوئی صورت نظر نہیں آتی

My hopes signal despair.
Troubles nest with me.

My death is by decree: why
Does sleep slip by me?

I have laughed at my lows.
Now nothing lifts me.

For perks I tried piety.
That life did not suit me.

Smell it, if you cannot see.
A heart burns inside me.

I am in a place where
No hint of I reaches me.

Is Ghalib off to Kaaba?
His nerve astonishes me.

16 – Perilous

آہ کو چاہیے اک عمر اثر ہوتے تک
کون جیتا ہے تری زلف کے سر ہوتے تک

A sigh takes forever to sway hearts.
How long before I untangle your curls?

The soul's sea journey is perilous.
How shall a drop make it to a pearl?

I grant you will not put off my plea: yet
I will be dust when you hear from me.

In a flash, the sun takes out the dew.
I too will go when he asks for me.

Nothing cures this agony but death.
A candle too burns until its last breath.

17 – Limits

ہوس کو ہے نشاطِ کار کیا کیا
نہ ہو مرنا تو جینے کا مزا کیا

Crossing limits makes us free.
We die to live dangerously.

Why singe my heart all day?
At once, pitch your bolt at me.

I surf the sea of ecstasy. Saqi,
Your snubs cannot sink me.

Each drop proclaims the sea.
What glory! He asks for me.

Ghalib, behold her artistry.
In each glance, what archery!

18 – Worship

بندگی میں بھی وہ آزادہ و خود بیں ہیں کہ ہم
الٹے پھر آئے درِ کعبہ اگر وا نہ ہوا

In worship too I am imperious, free.
I walked away when Kaaba shut me out.

So singular, only he sees himself. If you
Gaze at him, your eye shuts him out.

A grief contained migrates to a scar.
A drop perishes, if the sea shuts it out.

Seek the sea in a drop, sun in a spark.
Self-love is easy: try taking yourself out.

Word is out, Ghalib hangs tonight. I too
Was there: she did not take him out.

19 – Collar

گلہ ہے شوق کو دل میں بھی تنگیِ جا کا
گہر میں محو ہوا اضطراب دریا کا

Inside the heart, love carps it lacks space.
Inside a pearl, the raging sea is free.

Answering letters cramps your style.
I push my pen until I clinch my story.

I could not scale the peaks of light.
The old markers did not work for me.

Skipping the play, I let her collar me.
I played it safe: this love is haggle-free.

My tears are only tokens of my grief.
I hold back a flood wide as the sea.

A glaring sky takes me back to her.
On sultry days, she has no time for pity.

20 – Impaled

میں اور بزمِ مے سے یوں تشنہ کام آؤں
گر میں نے کی تھی توبہ ساقی کو کیا ہوا تھا

Although I had sworn to stay sober, Saqi,
I was at your party: and you let me go thirsty.

On one shaft, she has the two impaled.
Never was my head so close to my heart.

On your feet, Ghalib, figure this out. In
Good times, you had your life figured out.

21 – Confidant

ذکر اس پری وش کا اور پھر بیاں اپنا
بن گیا رقیب آخر تھا جو راز داں اپنا

She had beauty and she had my praise too.
I lost a confidant and *he* is courting her.

If I had a house the other side of the sky,
What could confine my art, my ardor?

My letters do nothing. I will go show her
My bloodied pen and blistered fingers.

My rivals will never tell on me again.
I got them to sign my screeds against her.

I had no lock on wit nor led in charisma.
Ghalib, how did I offend the higher powers?

22 – Sinai

گلہ ہے شوق کو دل میں بھی تنگیِ جا کا
گہر میں محو ہوا اضطراب دریا کا

Why did I not perish in the glow of that face?
Such awesome power in a lover is scary.

Sword in hand she arrives, wild to slay me.
My rage for dying will kill before she does.

My friend has quit tormenting me. She
Was livid, my gashes were lifting my spirits.

The blisters on my feet were vexing me of late.
At last, she is laying thorns on my path.

Let him direct his lightning at me, not Sinai.
The Saqi measures the wine to the cup.

It's Ghalib I see, bashing his head bloody,
Every time I walk past the ramparts of her house.

23 – Suitors

ہوئی تاخیر تو کچھ باعثِ تاخیر بھی تھا
آپ آتے تھے مگر کوئی عناں گیر بھی تھا

If a thing's delayed, there's a thing delaying it.
Not you, your suitors slowed you down a bit.

It wasn't right, pinning my troubles on you.
The furies, fate, kismet, each had a hand in it.

If you have forgotten, this was my address.
I was once your quarry and you were fond of it.

Captive, I stay awake, thinking of you all night.
It's true my shackled feet also hurt a bit.

I did not ask for this blinding flash of light.
I would hear him speak: my heart aches for it.

If she shrinks from coming too close to me,
She is a sharp shooter: an arrow too would do it.

Unfairly, we are tried on the word of angels.
Was there a man like us to say he saw us do it?

24.1 – Headstone

لازم تھا کہ دیکھو مرا رستا کوئی دن اور
تنہا گئے کیوں اب رہو تنہا کوئی دن اور

Go, fix your eyes on the road a few more days.
Gone alone, now wait alone a few more days.

Your headstone or my head, one has got to go.
Give me time to grieve – only a few more days.

Yesterday you came: now you declare, I *go*.
Once, let us agree, just a few more days?

It's good-bye & see you on Judgment Day?
Child, that *day* is now, not in a few more days.

Lord of eternity, Ärif was not yet thirty.
Why could *he* not have just a few more days?

I know you've hated me and Nayyar is a bore.
Just do it for the kids: stay back a few more days.

What fools they are to ask, Why does Ghalib live?
It's my fate. I must crave this life a few more days.

24.2 – Goodbye

لازم تھا کہ دیکھو مرا رستا کوئی دن اور
تنہا گئے کیوں اب رہو تنہا کوئی دن اور

I begged, wait for me: Did you?
I cannot cut short my days.

Head against headstone; thus
I will go, not in weeks but days.

Yesterday here: now, may I go?
For once, stay another day.

Goodbye, until the Last Day?
As if that day is not today.

God, you have eternity; yet he
Could not have an extra day.

No pushover, yet straight
You took the angel's Q&A.

We do not say, for us; for joy
Of kids, stay another day.

Only fools ask, Why do I live?
As God decrees, Ghalib obeys.

25.1 – Song

نہ گلِ نغمہ ہوں نہ پردۂ ساز
میں ہوں اپنی شکست کی آواز

No roseate song, no silk-spun melody.
I am the last echo of my own defeat.

Only I can watch you weaving lilacs in your hair.
I bought from all eyes the rights to your beauty.

No ordinary captive, love keeps me in this glade.
Wings spread, I will fly when the sky invites.

I wait for a time this side of life, when I
Draw out your beauty, not just dream of it.

Did you take heat for your kindness to me?
I am in need: and you the provider of needs.

25.2 – Grieving

نہ گلِ نغمہ ہوں نہ پردۂ ساز
میں ہوں اپنی شکست کی آواز

Not canticle nor music weaving.
Listen to my heart, grieving.

Such magic is her beauty,
Outlandish fears spook me.

Cold, sly, insouciant? Many
Gardens burn inside me.

If kind, did the earth shake?
You give because I receive.

He's gone: Asadullah Khan.
Sinner, lover: Ah what a man!

26 – Coyness

کل کے لیے کر آج نہ خِسّت شراب میں
یہ سوچے گمٹن ہے ساقی کوثر کے باب میں

Do not be miserly now for wine tomorrow.
He owns the vineyard: his Cup is never dry.

Once, you snapped at an angel when he
Scoffed at us. Why have we no honor today?

This horse flies at the touch: we ride
Without reins, going we know not where.

If seeker, seeking, sought are in their essence
One, how does the *One* know another?

Coyness is a screen that hides self from self.
Not from us, you are veiled from yourself.

The face you see in vision, *that* face is a mask.
You are still asleep though you wake in a dream.

27 – Shroud

بے نیازی حد سے گزری بندہ پرور کب تلک
ہم کہیں گے حالِ دل اور آپ فرماویں گے کیا

She hides behind the mask of coy indifference.
I cry, it hurts: she answers, it gets worse.

If my mentor comes calling, let him be my guest.
But if he breaks down, how do I handle him?

I will renew my suit, sword and shroud in hand.
If she refuses now, what will be her excuse?

If my friends shackle me, let them try this too.
Has anyone forced love to alter its ways?

She binds me forever in her silken coils.
I am love's captive: my beefs could be worse.

28 – Maelstrom

وا رستہ اس سے ہیں کہ محبّت ہی کیوں نہ ہو
کیجے ہمارے ساتھ عداوت ہی کیوں نہ ہو

I am done insisting this has to be love.
Save it for me if it's hating you do.

For every pestilence there is a cure.
Love is the exception: it takes no cure.

Man is by himself a maelstrom of ideas.
I always have company, alone, by myself.

I will be camping at her door tonight.
I am battle-ready: let her raise hell.

29 – Mercy

میں انہیں چھیڑوں اور کچھ نہ کہیں
چل نکلتے جو مے پیے ہوتے

I took liberties with her, got away with it.
Where would this go had she too been tipsy?

Are you nature's fury, a plague on my days?
Be what you will be: also be for me.

If he has allotted so much pain to me,
Why did he not give an extra heart too?

Ghalib, she too would have seen the light.
Why did you not stay for days of mercy?

30 – Uncoffined

دھمکی میں مر گیا جو نہ باب نبرد تھا
عشق نبرد پیشا طلب گار مرد تھا

He blanched, nearly died, at love's first swagger.
If love takes your head, surrender it, be free.

In silent arteries, time irrigates your flesh.
In this death-crafted life, we crave to be free.

Catch this fever once, it becomes your life.
The heart grows in pain till death sets you free.

My friends never found a cure for my rage.
Lashed to the cross, I walk the desert free.

In death, Ghalib lay uncoffined, unwashed.
May God bless the man. He dared to be free.

31 – Férhad

جز قیس اور کوئی نہ آیا بروۓ کار
صحرا مگر بہ تنگی چشمِ حسود تھا

Qays always played love's most exacting parts.
In the first act, his rivals took stage fright.

It was in a dream, but I had a life with her.
Awake, I am adjusting: there was nothing to it.

A white winding-sheet hides my blemishes.
No garments hid my shame until I came to this.

'They say, Férhad died of self-inflicted wounds.
A novice, he could not just drop dead.'

32.1 – Mentor

کہتے ہو نہ دینگے ہم دل اگر پڑا پایا
دل کہاں کہ تم کہتے ہم نے مدعا پایا

You say that you do not give back stray hearts.
If I still had one, I would be glad to lose it.

She is coy and cunning: sweet, exacting too.
She is playing you if you do not know it.

All that I know about my heart is this:
Every time I look for it, she says she has it.

My mentor's talk rubs salt in my wounds.
A losing game if he too gets nothing out of it.

32.2 – Registry

کہتے ہو نہ دینگے ہم دل اگر پڑا پایا
دل کہاں کہ تم کیجۓ ہم نے مدعاٰ پایا

She keeps a registry of hearts lost and stolen.
If I ever lose one I know where to find it.

Life's longest epic is a day in love. I traded
All my cares for one that takes no cure.

In life she is laid back, in love enigmatic.
She only plays cool: she is aching for you.

A session with my analyst disorients me.
A job well-done! What does it do for him?

33 – Fire

دل مرا سوزِ نہاں سے بے محابا جل گیا
آتشِ خاموش کے مانند گویا جل گیا

It was a fire unlike any I have seen. It went
To work inwardly: the heat was extreme.

There is nothing I could save: a memory,
A face. All that I had was lost in this blaze.

Every wound, every scar was a radiant star.
This festival of lights was lost in a blaze.

Ghalib, I seek solace in ruins and ashes,
A desert set apart from false painted faces.

34 – Love-Crazed

سراپا رہنِ عشق و نا گزیرِ الفتِ ہستی
عبادت برق کی کرتا ہوں اور افسوس حاصل کا

Love-crazed yet craving life. I worship fire
But recant when lightning finds me out.

If your cup overflows, my thirst is deep.
Drinking makes me sober, Saqi try me out.

35.1 – Artist

نقش فریادی ہے کس کی شوخیِ تحریر کا
کاغذی ہے پیرہن ہر پیکرِ تصویر کا

Where is the Artist whose art they protest? Every
Prop, every player, dreads his part in the play.

Hard, it is hard, digging through granite nights.
It takes a thousand sparks to break into day.

The heat is intense when lovers pine for death.
When she lifts her sword, the edge strips away.

Go, catch my drift with nets of finest weave.
The arc of my flight will take your breath away.

My foot shackles melt like braids cast in fire.
Ghalib, I tread embers to pass my prison days.

35.2 – Rock

نقش فریادی ہے کس کی شوخیِ تحریر کا
کاغذی ہے پیرہن ہر پیکرِ تصویر کا

Are we in his story for comic relief?
Cosmic players cry, as they stew.

Inside a rock we wake each night,
Digging our way back to you.

She polishes her storied sword.
Will it draw blood or gather dew?

Your epistemic nets have holes
So huge, the simurgh slips through.

Ghalib, cast your cold conceits
In love's fire till death delivers you.

35.3 – Sword

نقش فریادی ہے کس کی شوخیِ تحریر کا
کاغذی ہے پیرہن ہر پیکرِ تصویر کا

He scripts, scores, directs the play. Casting
Complete, he reads the lines too. We lip sync.

Cliff hanging is hard. From rock to rock we
Climb all night, dying for a look at you.

When she lifts her sword, mad lovers
Make her day: they have the spunk to die.

Stretch everywhere the cunning meshes
You weave. I weave a finer mesh for you.

Ghalib, a wild fire goes everywhere I go.
A frenzy feeds this fire: in prison I am free.

35.4 – Beauty

نقش فریادی ہے کس کی شوخیِ تحریر کا
کاغذی ہے پیرہن ہر پیکرِ تصویر کا

Shaped for eternity: yet tied to time's cross.
What did he think whose hand crafted us?

Night after night he left us in the dark.
How could we stay true if he eluded us?

The edge of her sword leaps at us.
For beauty we bled, till death uplifted us.

Their clever snares never caught us.
Cold logic they had but never charted us.

In a solitary cell, Ghalib, we tread fire.
In body, heart, and soul time has tested us.

35.5 – Galaxies

نقش فریادی ہے کس کی شوخیِ تحریر کا
کاغذی ہے پیرہن ہر پیکرِ تصویر کا

The galaxies grieve,
Whose whimsy are we?

Inside a cage he cries,
It's godawful lonely.

We are true lovers
At the sword's mercy.

No spy can find us.
Only *he* knows me.

Unfree, Ghalib carps,
Dare you hold me?

Notes on the Translations

Ghazal #, Sh'er #
Title

1, 4
Afterlife   Khizer: variously described in Islamic traditions
as guide, saint and prophet, endowed with eternal life.
Some traditions identify him with Moses' teacher and
traveling companion mentioned in the Qur'an.

22, 5
Sinai   Saqi: cup-bearer, male or female; one who serves wine in
a tavern or a private assembly. In Urdu poetry, wine, the
prohibited drink, often serves as a metaphor for the ecsta-
sy of union with a human or divine beloved. It makes
sense to capitalize Saqi, especially when the poet address-
es him/her in the ghazal.

24.1, 6
Headstone   Angel's Q&A: In Islamic tradition, an angel questions the
dead in the grave about his/her faith and deeds.
Nayyar was a friend of Ghalib. He cherished the late Ärif,
Ghalib's nephew, whose death this ghazal commemorates.

25.2, 5
Grieving   Asadullah Khan is the poet's name; Ghalib is his poetic
name.

26, 2
Coyness   Second sh'er: In the Qur'an, when God asks the angels to
bow before Adam, one of the angels (according to one
reading) refuses and is banished from His presence.

35.2, 4
Rock   Simurgh: a mythical bird-like creature in Persian poetry,
long-lived and full of wisdom. Farid Uddin Attar, a sufi
poet, has used the Simurgh as a metaphor for God.

About the Translator

M. Shahid Alam is Professor of Economics at Northeastern University. His translations from the Urdu of Ghalib have appeared in numerous periodicals, including *Blackbird, The Critical Muslim, Kenyon Review, Prairie Schooner, The Southern Review, TriQuarterly,* and *Western Humanities Review.* Alam is the author of *Poverty from the Wealth of Nations* and *Governments and Markets in Economic Development Strategies.*

About Orison Books

Orison Books is a 501(c)3 non-profit literary press focused on the life of the spirit from a broad and inclusive range of perspectives. We seek to publish books of exceptional poetry, fiction, and non-fiction from perspectives spanning the spectrum of spiritual and religious thought, ethnicity, gender identity, and sexual orientation.

As a non-profit literary press, Orison Books depends on the support of donors. To find out more about our mission and our books, or to make a donation, please visit www.orisonbooks.com.